# The Nature Kid's Guide to ORANGUTANS

## DAVID ANDERSON

LP Media Inc. Publishing
Text copyright © 2026 by LP Media Inc.
All rights reserved.



For information address LP Media Inc. Publishing,
30012 Variolite St NW, Princeton MN 55371
www.lpmedia.org

Publication Data

Orangutans
The Nature Kid's Guide to Orangutans — First edition.

Summary: "Learn all about Orangutans, the Nature Kid Way"
— Provided by publisher.

ISBN: 979-8-89818-129-1

[1. Orangutans - Non-Fiction] I. Title.

Title: The Nature Kid's Guide to Orangutans

# CONTENTS

# TREETOP HOMES

## Rustle! An orangutan climbs high and grabs a branch.

Orangutans live in rainforests. They spend most of their time in trees. The forest **canopy** is their home.

Rainforests are warm and wet all year long. Rain falls almost every day. This makes the trees grow very tall and close together. Thick vines and branches connect the treetops like bridges. Orangutans use these to swing from tree to tree without ever touching the ground

Trees give orangutans everything they need. They find food in the branches. Leaves also keep them dry when it rains. The treetops are safe places to rest.

ISLAND
APES

## Hoot! An orangutan swings through leaves. The island is misty.

Orangutans live on two islands. The islands are Borneo and Sumatra. Both are in Southeast Asia.

Borneo is the bigger island. Most orangutans live there. Sumatra is smaller, but it has orangutans too.

These islands are hot, wet, and full of rainforests. Rain falls almost every day. This makes rainforests grow. It is the perfect place for orangutans to live.

**Borneo is the third largest island in the world. It is about the size of Texas!**

# BIG BODIES

# Thump! A big orangutan lands on a thick branch. He swings through the trees.

Orangutans are the largest animals that live in trees. Males are much bigger than females and can weigh up to 200 pounds!

Females are smaller, usually weighing about 90 pounds. Their lighter bodies help them climb thin branches.

Males have wide, flat faces called **flanges**. These cheek pads make their faces look very big. They also grow long beards.

**A male orangutan's face flanges never stop growing. The older he gets, the bigger they get!**

# AMAZING ARMS

An orangutan's arms are about one and a half times longer than its legs.

## Stretch! An orangutan reaches far with one long arm.

Orangutans have the longest arms of all the great apes. Their arm span can reach over 7 feet wide. That is longer than most adults are tall!

Their arms are about seven times stronger than a human's. Orangutans use them to hang from branches. They can hold their whole body with just one arm.

Their hands work like hooks. Long, curved fingers wrap around branches tightly. This grip keeps them safe high in the trees. Their arms are perfect for forest life.

# SUPER SENSES

**Sniff! An orangutan smells a ripe fruit nearby. She looks up to find it.**

Orangutans have sharp senses that help them survive. Their eyes see colors very well. This helps them spot ripe fruit hiding among the green leaves.

Their noses are useful too. Orangutans can smell fruit from far away, even before they can see it.

They also have good hearing. They listen for other orangutans calling through the forest. Together, these senses help them find food and stay safe.

Orangutans can remember where fruit trees are for years!

STAY SAFE

**Crack! A branch snaps below. An orangutan stays still and quiet.**

Orangutans stay safe by being careful. They move slowly and quietly through the trees. This helps them avoid danger below.

Their red-brown fur blends in with the forest. Shadows and leaves hide them from predators. Staying high up keeps them away from tigers.

Orangutans are very smart. They watch and wait when something seems wrong. Being patient and careful keeps them safe.

Orangutans spend about 95% of their time in trees. They rarely ever touch ground!

FRUIT
FANS

**Chomp! An orangutan bites into a juicy fig. Yum! This is her favorite snack.**

Orangutans love fruit more than any other food. Fruit makes up more than half of what they eat. Figs are one of their favorites.

They also eat leaves, bark, and insects. Sometimes they find honey or bird eggs too.

Orangutans remember where fruit trees grow. They also know when each tree has ripe fruit. They will travel back to the trees exactly when their fruits are ripest.

Orangutans will eat over 400 different kinds of foods!

# LONG CALLS

FUN
FACT!
A male orangutan's long call can
be heard up to 2 miles away!

**Howl! A male orangutan makes a loud, long call that echoes through the forest.**

Male orangutans make very loud calls. These calls can last up to 10 minutes. Other orangutans hear them from over a mile away.

The calls sound like roars and rumbles. Males have large throat sacs that make the sound louder. These sacs fill with air like balloons.

Long calls tell other males to stay away. Females listen for these calls to find strong mates.

Orangutans also make softer sounds like squeaks and grunts to communicate up close.

WATCH OUT

## Growl! A tiger walks below. An orangutan stays very still.

Orangutans have a few **predators**. Sumatran tigers hunt them on the ground. This is why orangutans stay high in trees.

But some predators can climb. Clouded leopards hunt young orangutans in trees. Large pythons are a danger up high too.

Adult orangutans are big and strong. Most predators leave them alone. But babies and young orangutans face the most risk.

**Mother orangutans will break off tree branches and throw them at predators below to protect their babies!**

# HIDE HIGH

**Swoosh! An orangutan swings up fast. She climbs a thick tree.**

Orangutans climb high to stay safe. They spend most of their time far above the ground. This keeps them away from tigers and other predators.

They know how to hide in the forest. Thick leaves make good cover. If they spot danger, orangutans make a loud kiss-squeak sound.

Mothers teach babies where to go. Young orangutans learn the safest routes.

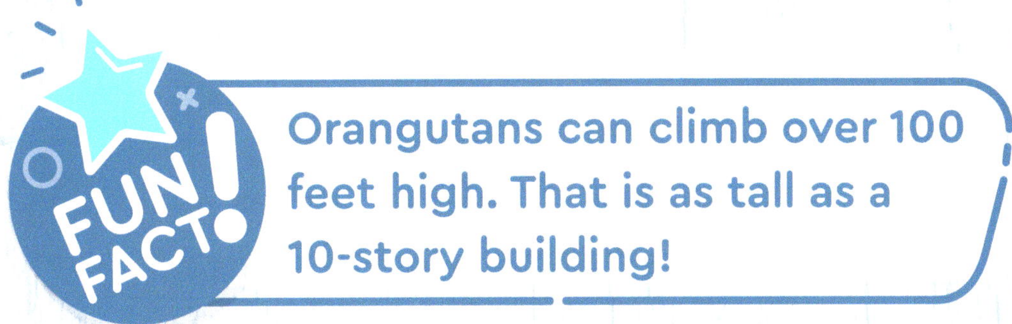


Orangutans can climb over 100 feet high. That is as tall as a 10-story building!

SWING TIME

# Swing! A young orangutan grabs a vine and swings to the next tree.

Orangutans are some of the world's most amazing climbers. They glide through trees using both their hands and feet. Their long fingers can grip branches like hooks.

They will swing from branch to branch. This is called **brachiating**. Orangutans can travel far and fast without touching the ground.

Young orangutans learn by watching their mothers. By age three, they climb on their own.

Orangutans can swing through trees at speeds up to 35 miles per hour!

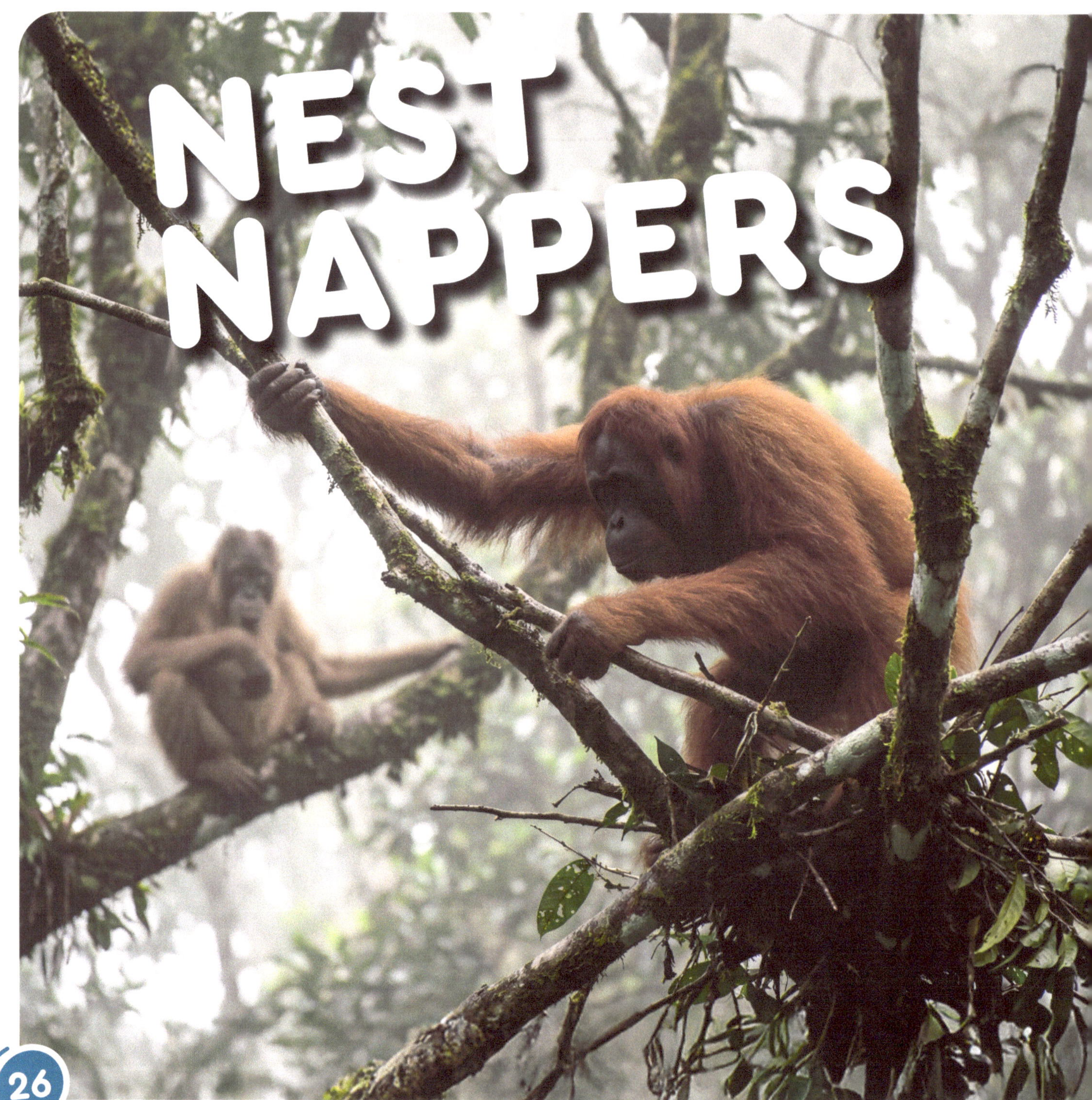


NEST
NAPPERS

## Snap! An orangutan bends branches together. She builds a cozy bed.

Orangutans build nests every day. They bend branches together to make a soft bed. Each nest takes about ten minutes to build.

They sleep in their nests at night. Sometimes they nap during the day too. Orangutans make a new nest almost every night.

Mothers share nests with their babies. By age three, young orangutans start practicing how to build their own.

Orangutans may build over 30,000 nests in their lifetime. They sometimes even add leafy pillows!

# SOLO STARS

**Grunt! A male orangutan sits alone. He quietly eats fruit all by himself.**

Orangutans live alone most of the time. They are one of the most **solitary** great apes. Adult males spend almost all their days by themselves.

Females are different. Mothers stay with their babies for up to 10 years.

Orangutans may meet at fruit trees. They eat near each other for a brief time, then go their separate ways.

Male orangutans have large home ranges. One male's home range can cover up to 15 square miles!

FINDING LOVE
30

## Squeak! A female orangutan calls softly from a tall tree.

Orangutans do not live in pairs. Males and females only spend time together for a few days during mating season.

Males make a loud booming call to attract females. It can be heard almost a mile away through the thick forest. The male's big cheek flanges help make the sound even louder.

Females have babies about once every eight years. This is the longest time between babies of any land mammal!

A male orangutan's long call can last up to four minutes. Other males hear it and stay far away!

# BABY TIME

DID YOU KNOW?
Baby orangutans stay with their mothers for up to 8 years. That's as old as a third grader!

## Grab on! A tiny baby orangutan holds tight to its mother.

Baby orangutans are born with pink skin around their eyes and mouths. Their faces turn darker as they grow older.

Newborns weigh about 3 to 4 pounds. They are very small and helpless. Babies cannot let go of their mothers at first. They hold on tight to their mother's fur as she climbs through the trees

Infants drink their mother's milk. Then they start eating soft fruit around four months old.

Young orangutans are very playful. They hang from branches, tumble around, and wrestle with each other. Playing helps them build the strong arms they will need to swing through the trees.

# MAMA KNOWS

DID YOU KNOW?
Mother orangutans can carry babies weighing up to 30 pounds!

**Snort! A mother orangutan gently grooms her baby high in the trees.**

Mother orangutans are amazing parents. They carry their babies everywhere for the first two years. Young ones cling to their mother's belly or back.

Mothers teach their babies everything. They show them which fruits are safe to eat. They also teach them how to build sleeping nests.

Young orangutans watch and copy their mothers. They learn to use sticks as tools.

At night, mothers and babies share a nest. They stay warm and safe together.

FORESTS
FALLING

## Rumble! Big machines knock down trees. An orangutan watches from above.

Orangutans are in great danger. Their habitat is disappearing.  People cut down forests to make farms. They grow palm oil trees. Palm oil is in many foods and soaps.

When trees fall, orangutans lose their homes. They have nowhere to go.

Forest fires also hurt them. Fires destroy the places where they live.

Over 100,000 Bornean orangutans have been lost since 1999. Scientists worry they could go extinct in just 50 years.

HELPING
HANDS

# Click! A scientist takes a photo. She counts orangutans.

Many people are trying to help save orangutans. Scientists study them in the wild. They learn what orangutans need.

Some groups protect forests. They stop people from cutting trees. This keeps orangutans safe.

Rescue centers help hurt orangutans. Workers teach young orphans to climb. They teach them to find food.

With all these peoples help, we can save the orangutans!

**Some rescue centers have set free over 500 orangutans. These orangutans now live in safe forests.**

# GLOSSARY

### canopy
The top layer of a forest where tree branches and leaves spread out like a roof.

### solitary
Living alone instead of in a group.

### brachiating
Swinging from branch to branch using your arms.

### flanges
Wide, flat cheek pads that grow on the faces of male orangutans.

### predators
Animals that hunt and eat other animals.